DRONES
EYES IN THE SKIES

MILITARY DRONES

DANIEL R. FAUST

PowerKiDS press.

New York

Published in 2016 by The Rosen Publishing Group, Inc.
29 East 21st Street, New York, NY 10010

First Edition

Editor: Sarah Machajewski
Book Design: Reann Nye

Photo Credits: Cover, p. 1 HIGH-G Productions/Stocktrek Images/Getty Images; p. 5 Claude Paris/ AP Images; p. 6 Roger Viollet/Getty Images; p. 7 https://commons.wikimedia.org/wiki/File-Teledyne-Ryan-Firebee-hatzerim-1.jpg; p. 8 Eugene Berman/Shutterstock.com; p. 9 https://commons.wikimedia.org/ wiki/File-Tadiran-Mastiff-III-hatzerim-1.jpg; pp. 11, 12, 13 Ethan Miller/Getty Images News/Getty Images; p. 15 (background) mexrix/Shutterstock.com; p. 16 https://commons.wikimedia.org/wiki/File-Black_Hornet_Nano_Helicopter_UAV.jpg; p. 17 https://commons.wikimedia.org/wiki/File-24th_MEU_in_Djibouti_for_sustainment_training_150331-M-YH418-001.jpg; p. 18 https://commons.wikimedia.org/wiki/File-Shadow_200_UAV_(2).jpg; p. 19 (top) https://commons.wikimedia.org/wiki/File:Global_Hawk_1.jpg; p. 19 (bottom) https://commons.wikimedia.org/wiki/File-RQ-4_Global_Hawk_3.jpg; p. 21 Christian Science Monitor/Getty Images; p. 23 http://aircraft.wikia.com/wiki/File-800px-RQ-2_Pioneer_on_launch_rail_1.JPEG; p. 25 https://commons.wikimedia.org/wiki/File-%27Devils%27_take_to_the_skies_140821-A-XQ797-728.jpg; p. 27 MANJUNATH KIRAN/AFP/Getty Images; p. 29 Getty Images/Getty Images News/Getty Images; p. 30 Erik Simonsen/Photographer's Choice/ Getty Images.

Library of Congress Cataloging-in-Publication Data

Faust, Daniel R., author.
 Military drones / Daniel R. Faust.
     pages cm. — (Drones: eyes in the skies)
 Includes index.
ISBN 978-1-5081-4496-0 (pbk.)
ISBN 978-1-5081-4497-7 (6 pack)
ISBN 978-1-5081-4498-4 (library binding)
1. Drone aircraft—United States—Juvenile literature. I. Title.
UG1242.D7F38 2016
 355.8'3—dc23
                          2015032562

Manufactured in the United States of America

CPSIA Compliance Information: Batch #BW16PK: For Further Information contact Rosen Publishing, New York, New York at 1-800-237-9932

CONTENTS

DRONES ARE EVERYWHERE!

Stories about drones are in the news every day. Drones, or unmanned aerial **vehicles** (UAVs), are aircraft that don't carry a human pilot. Drones are controlled remotely by a human operator, although some drones can be programmed for **autonomous** flight.

Most drones are used by the military and **intelligence** agencies such as the Central Intelligence Agency (CIA) and National Security Administration (NSA). Law enforcement organizations also use drones. **Recreational** drones called quadcopters have become a popular hobby for people of all ages. The entertainment industry has started using camera-equipped drones on some film and television sets. Even Amazon and Google have investigated whether or not drones can be used to deliver packages. Although drones are quickly becoming common in everyday life, most people still think of them as military **technology**.

One day, the skies may be filled with fleets of drones operated by companies such as Amazon and Google. Until then, most drones are operated by the military and government agencies.

THE FIRST DRONES

Drones may seem like brand-new technology, but the idea has been around for more than 150 years. In 1849, Austria launched 200 pilotless balloons armed with bombs to drop on the city of Venice. Balloons were also used during the American Civil War. Both the Union and the Confederacy used balloons for **reconnaissance** and to drop bombs on enemy targets. During the Spanish-American War, the U.S. military used a kite-mounted camera to take the first aerial reconnaissance photographs in history.

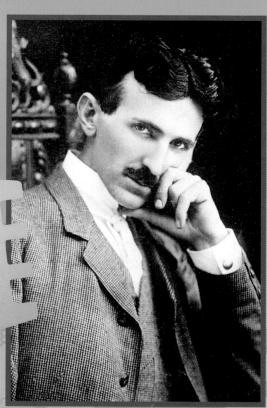

NIKOLA TESLA

Inventor Nikola Tesla was the first person to successfully control a vehicle using a radio signal. In 1898, he used radio waves to control a boat on a pond in New York's Madison Square Garden.

The Ryan Firebee, such as the one pictured here, was one of the first jet-propelled drones.

Pilotless vehicles were used in the early 20th century as training targets for pilots and antiaircraft gunners. Self-propelled torpedoes dropped from aircraft were used during World War I and World War II. The modern drone was first developed during the Vietnam War.

During the Vietnam War, the U.S. Air Force began planning to use unmanned aircraft. The military was concerned about losing pilots over enemy territory. When the Soviet Union shot down an American U-2 spy plane in 1960, it became clear an alternative to manned aircraft was needed.

LOCKHEED U-2 DRAGON LADY

Before drones, manned aircraft like the Lockheed U-2 flew reconnaissance missions over enemy territory. In 1960, a U-2 was shot down over the Soviet Union and the pilot, Gary Powers, was taken prisoner.

DRONE EVOLUTION

The earliest drones were used as training targets. Later drones were used for **surveillance**. The newest drones are weapons that can attack targets.

ISRAELI TADIRAN MASTIFF

Technological advances in radio, video, and computers in the 1950s and 1960s made unmanned aerial vehicles a reality. Now it was possible to fly over enemy territory to gather intelligence without risking a pilot's life. The first modern battlefield drone was the Tadiran Mastiff. It was the first UAV to provide real-time live streaming video. Today, military drones are used by at least 50 countries, including the United States, Israel, and China.

GETTING IN THE AIR

Some military drones are small enough to be launched by hand. Other drones require the use of a runway, just like a regular airplane. Some drones need to be launched from special catapult-like devices. Once in the air, drones use simple flight computers and navigational equipment such as GPS to **stabilize** themselves and avoid obstacles.

Depending on what kind of drone it is, operators can control drones from the ground, much like a radio-controlled airplane. They can also control drones from a location that's hundreds or thousands of miles away. Operators use remote controls, which look like the controllers for your favorite gaming system. Some drones are controlled from a central control center filled with computer stations and video monitors. They're called ground control stations (GCS).

Although the U.S. military uses drones all over the world, many of them are controlled remotely by operators at military bases in the United States.

EYES IN THE SKY

Reconnaissance and surveillance have always been the main uses for military drones. Military drones have still cameras and video cameras, as well as lowlight, infrared, and radar capabilities. These features allow drones to operate at night and during poor weather conditions. Because they don't carry human pilots, drones can operate 24 hours a day, seven days a week.

The cameras on military drones can take pictures during the day and at night. This image was taken during a test flight.

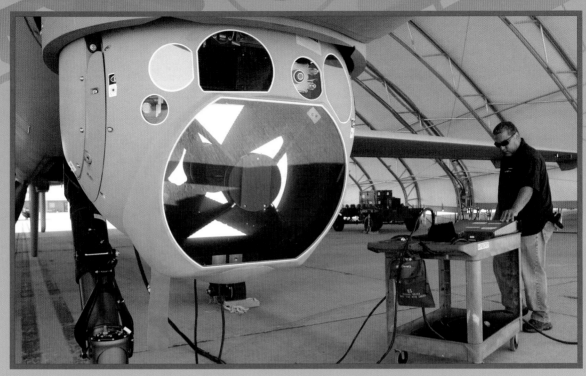

Spy drones provide a valuable service to both military and intelligence operations. Drones can hover for hours or even days over enemy territory. They can circle an area continuously, providing full-color, real-time video of enemy troops. These aircraft can provide our troops with valuable information so they can plan and act accordingly. Intelligence agencies and law enforcement also use surveillance drones to search for and track **terrorists** and criminals.

SKUNK WORKS

"Skunk Works" is the nickname for Lockheed Martin's Advanced Development Programs. Skunk Works is responsible for some of the most advanced aircraft in the world, including drones.

SEARCH AND DESTROY

After the September 11 terrorist attacks in 2001 and the start of the War on Terror in 2003, it became clear the U.S. military wasn't prepared to fight an **unconventional** war. Even if the military could locate a target, it might not be possible for soldiers to get to it. If a drone could be used to gather intelligence, maybe it could also be used for more **offensive** missions.

Drones used in combat situations are called unmanned combat air vehicles, or UCAVs. They're also commonly called hunter-killers. Combat drones are usually armed with missiles and bombs as well as the computers needed to fire them. Because they need to carry heavy weaponry, combat drones can be as large as a regular aircraft.

COMBAT DRONE

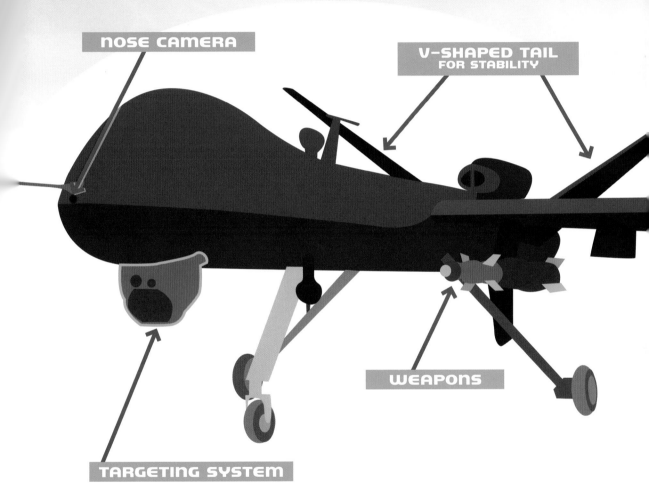

NOSE CAMERA

V–SHAPED TAIL
FOR STABILITY

TARGETING SYSTEM

WEAPONS

Hunter-killer drones like the MQ-9 Reaper are built for combat. They have all the equipment needed to locate and attack their targets.

THE U.S. MILITARY DRONE FLEET

The U.S. Air Force uses many kinds of aircraft. About one-third of its fleet is made of drones. Military drones come in all different shapes and sizes. Some drones are small enough to fit in the palm of your hand, while others are as large as full-sized airplanes.

BLACK HORNET NANO

The U.S. military began testing the Black Hornet Nano in March 2015. It's one of the smallest drones in the world—small enough to be carried in your pocket. Drones of this size are called microUAVs or nanoUAVs.

The smallest drones used by the military, such as the Black Hornet and the Raven, are small enough to be carried and launched by hand.

RQ-11B RAVEN

The RQ-11B Raven weighs about 4 pounds (1.8 kg) and looks like a model airplane. This small drone is launched by hand and can also be programmed to operate autonomously. The Raven is used mainly to provide aerial footage to troops that are moving through a city.

DEFENSE ADVANCED RESEARCH PROJECTS AGENCY (DARPA)

DARPA is an agency within the U.S. Department of Defense. It's responsible for designing and developing advanced technology for the U.S. military.

The medium-sized RQ-7 Shadow is about the size of a person. The Shadow can be flown almost 80 miles (129 km) away from its operator and can provide real-time video footage of a battlefield.

RQ-7 SHADOW

Larger drones, like the RQ-7 Shadow and the MQ-9 Reaper, can fly higher and stay in the air longer than smaller, handheld drones. Many of the larger drones carry weapons.

The most **iconic** drones in the U.S. military's fleet are the MQ-1 Predator and the MQ-9 Reaper. When you see a news story about drones, these are probably the drones that are pictured. The Predator and the Reaper are usually armed and used for combat missions called drone strikes.

RQ-4 GLOBAL HAWK

One of the largest drones used by the military is the RQ-4 Global Hawk. The Global Hawk weighs nearly 15,000 pounds (6,804 kg) and has a **wingspan** that measures 130 feet (40 m). These giants can fly as high as 60,000 feet (18,288 m) and can stay in the air for almost a day and a half.

MQ-9 REAPER

FATHER OF MODERN DRONES

It took a **visionary** to turn unreliable, remote-controlled aircraft into the most advanced military tool in use today. That visionary is an aircraft designer named Abraham Karem. Karem was born in Baghdad, Iraq, on June 27, 1937. His family moved to Israel in 1951. As a child, Karem was interested in **engineering** and model airplanes. He graduated with a degree in aircraft engineering and built his first drone for the Israeli Air Force in 1973.

In the late 1970s, Karem moved to the United States. He started a company called Leading Systems, Inc. Leading Systems would eventually be bought by General Atomics, which is a company that specializes in the aircraft and defense industries. General Atomics employed Karem to design a new UAV that would eventually become the Predator.

Karem's designs for the Predator included a new, quieter engine. This new kind of drone changed the way UAVs were used in military operations.

FAMOUS DRONE MISSIONS

While military drones have been in use since the Vietnam War, drone missions became increasingly common toward the end of the 20th century. The Persian Gulf War, which began in 1990, was the first conflict to see widespread use of drones in **tactical** operations. In 1999, NATO and the **Pentagon** used drones to locate and track targets on the ground during the Kosovo War.

After September 11, 2001, drones played an important role in the War on Terror. Drones were used to gather intelligence and locate enemy forces in Pakistan and Afghanistan. They were used to help capture former Libyan dictator Muammar Gaddafi in 2011. The Navy SEAL team responsible for finding Osama bin Laden relied on intelligence provided by drones.

WHAT IS NATO?

Created after World War II, the North Atlantic Treaty Organization (NATO) is an organization of 28 nations. Its purpose is to protect its members' safety and freedom.

During the Persian Gulf War, drones such as this RQ-2 Pioneer filled the skies over the Middle East. Pioneer drones were also used during the Kosovo War.

BENEFITS OF DRONE USE

There are many reasons why militaries use drones. Drones can fly 24 hours a day and in the worst weather conditions. Because they don't have to carry a human pilot, drones can fly higher than manned aircraft. They're also difficult for the enemy to detect and hard to shoot down. Perhaps the biggest benefit to using drones is they can save lives.

The U.S. military first started using drones to prevent the death of human pilots. Drones continue to be used for dangerous, high-risk missions instead of manned aircraft. Drones also save lives on the ground. Intelligence gathered by drones helps soldiers on the ground identify targets and avoid civilian **casualties**.

In the field, U.S. soldiers rely on the information gathered by reconnaissance drones to locate their targets and avoid dangerous situations.

LIVING UNDER DRONES

There are pros and cons to any technology. Drones are no different. Drones may save lives, but that doesn't mean they're perfect. Drones might look like robots out of a science-fiction movie, but they're controlled by human operators—and humans make mistakes.

Many people say combat drones kill more civilians than they save. Drones play a huge role in the War on Terror, and terrorists often hide in large groups of innocent people. In order to get their target, drones have often attacked places such as markets and private homes. People in countries such as Pakistan and Afghanistan have learned to live in fear of U.S. drones, afraid that they could be accidentally targeted by a drone strike at any time.

Drones often fly over the Middle East, including Afghanistan, which is pictured here. Some drones take pictures, while others are used in attacks. Innocent people are often harmed by drones used in this way.

OTHER USES FOR MILITARY DRONES

Predator and Reaper drones may be what most people think of when it comes to drones, but there are plenty of uses for the other kinds of military drones. Many drones used by the CIA gather intelligence rather than fight missions. The CIA uses this intelligence in order to protect the United States' national security.

To perform this duty, the CIA has a large fleet of combat drones that fly all over the world. Some people question whether the CIA should have its own fleet of armed drones. They also question if the drone program should be run by the Pentagon. Domestic law enforcement organizations, such as the FBI and Homeland Security, frequently use unarmed drones to patrol the skies over the United States.

This may look like the kind of drone used by the military, but it's actually operated by the Department of Homeland Security. Several law enforcement agencies use drones to protect our country's borders and search for criminals.

DRONES OF TOMORROW

It's unlikely the military is going to stop using drones any time soon. In fact, as drones become more common, we'll most likely see huge advances in drone technology. The U.S. military is currently working on several new kinds of drones to use in the future. One day, the military could be able to release swarms of insect-sized drones over enemy territory.

The military is also testing a helicopter-like drone that could hover over the battlefield. The U.S. Navy is experimenting with underwater drones that can be launched from submarines. They're also developing drones that can operate both in the air and underwater. The military is even trying to develop a flying aircraft carrier, which is a large aircraft that can launch and recover drones. Only time will tell what becomes of military drone technology.

GLOSSARY

autonomous: Operating on its own.

casualty: A death.

engineering: A branch of science that involves building and designing objects that improve our world.

iconic: Very famous or well-known.

intelligence: Information that is of military or political value.

offensive: Meant for use in an attack.

Pentagon: The headquarters of the U.S. Department of Defense.

reconnaissance: Observation of a region to locate an enemy.

recreational: Having to do with having fun.

stabilize: To steady.

surveillance: Close observation.

tactical: Done to support a military operation.

technology: Tools and the way people use them.

terrorist: A person who uses violence and fear to cause political change.

unconventional: Not usual.

vehicle: A machine that is powered to move on its own.

visionary: Someone who plans for the future with imagination or uncommon thinking.

wingspan: The measurement from the tip of one wing to the tip of the other.

INDEX

WEBSITES

Due to the changing nature of Internet links, PowerKids Press has developed an online list of websites related to the subject of this book. This site is updated regularly. Please use this link to access the list: www.powerkidslinks.com/dron/mili